Jake Adventures of a Greyhound

by

Jane Goldsmith

authorHOUSE®

AuthorHouse™ UK Ltd.
500 Avebury Boulevard
Central Milton Keynes, MK9 2BE
www.authorhouse.co.uk
Phone: 08001974150

First published by AuthorHouse 2/19/2008

ISBN: 978-1-4343-6498-2 (sc)

Printed in the United States of America
Bloomington, Indiana

This book is printed on acid-free paper.

Jake was adopted by the Goldsmith family and lives in Bedfordshire. Jane Goldsmith spent a year in France working with Sloughis (Arabian Greyhounds) in 1975. The owner of the dogs, Dr.Marie-Dominique De Caprona, is now a top breeder of the Sloughi in the USA. Jane thanks Dominique for the introduction to her lifelong love of sight hounds.

Thanks to Daisy Kay-Taylor, trustee for Greyhound Rescue West of England, for her help and editing

In hounds, hawks, arms and love

for every joy a hundred sorrows

Gace De La Vigne (14th century)

1

The first two years of my life are a mixture of vague memories. I do know that I was born to run, along with my brothers and sisters. Not only to run but to race. I had a number tattooed on the inside of my ear at some stage of my early existence to register me as a racing Greyhound. I am a member of that ancient noble breed, bred initially to hunt. My father was a black dog who had some success on the racetrack, my mother was black, my sister was black, but I am a handsome golden brindle. For me though, I soon decided that running after a small fluffy toy was a mug's game. I looked on in disbelief as my kennel mates, dressed up in brightly coloured jackets, ran around in a giant circle with creatures of a tall two-legged variety cheering them on. What were they thinking of? I just couldn't see the point of all that effort, impinging as it did on precious sleep time. I was fed whether I bothered to run or not, so I didn't bother.

From the start I fought with the other newborns for my food and my place. I was stronger than the two weaklings, but weaker than the big brother. I struggled to get enough, and that was my first lesson. There would always be a place to fight for, always a hierarchy in the pack, and always a leader of the pack. I found my place, but never lost my fear of lack of food. I gobbled it as quickly as possible in case one of the others got it before me or took it from me. That's how it is; food is the most important thing in life. Or maybe sleep. No, definitely food; and then sleep. Anyway, it's not that I did not like to run. I would have liked to run free and play, but there was none of that, it was all about training and racing.

So I can only describe a hazy impression of a row of kennels, a lot of noise, a few scraps with other tiresome dogs, and two-legged tyrants trying to get me to run fast. That's maybe a bit unfair. The two legs were fine, what little I had to do with them.

Most of the Greyhounds seemed to like the racing. There were some real competitive types, some a lot faster than me, and I do understand what they feel. I have felt the blood of my ancestors in my veins. Far in the future from where my story now begins I did run free and hunted deer on one occasion. I have run circles around other dogs and shown off my muscle, speed and skill. But I ran when I wanted to and not on command. I don't much like being forced into things.

Whoever bred me owned me or raced me soon got tired of me and my unenthusiastic and rebellious attitude. I was a failure as far as they were concerned, but actually I just didn't want to play the game. All I ever really wanted was a quiet life.

Eventually they gave me to a pack of the tall two-legged creatures that, I have to say, seem to all want to be top dog. From what little I can now recall, I went to a large building where everyone lived together. There were little and large two legged creatures living there and, well, it was a shock to say the least. I was still very young and had known nothing but kennels. Everything about it was strange and they seemed to expect me to know what to do. I missed the other dogs; after all I had not ever lived in such close contact with the tall beasts. When darkness came they would all disappear up this steep hill in the middle of the building and leave me alone. The space I had was much bigger than a cell at the kennels and I was afraid to start with. I would never go up the hill where they disappeared to, it was very scary. I did learn that they expected me to pee outside, but never really understood why and sometimes forgot. At first I was so nervous that I occasionally messed as well. This was not popular but I did not understand why.

The food was alright, which was the most important thing I suppose, and I had a much nicer bed than before. They did try to be kind and gave me a lot of petting and attention. But the young of the pack were so noisy and seemed to want to smother me, and I spent most of my time trying to get to my bed out of their way. But the real trouble was that they had one of the little bundles of fur creatures. Not like the ones at the track which weren't really alive anyway. I have learnt by now that they go by the name of cat. I loathe those scratchy little things, and anyway, I had been trained to chase small furry things, and yet here they got mad if I went after the stupid cat.

The cat teased and taunted me. It would stand and stare at me with its back arched and tail wagging slowly in a challenging fashion. It was quick though, I'll give it that. As I made my move towards it, it would take off like a dart and leap up somewhere high out of reach and look down on me haughtily from on high. It drove me mad. The rest of the time it was either outside or kept out of my way. The tall creatures doted on it. It sat with them on their big comfy sofa and chairs. I tried once to get on to the big sofa and was swiftly brushed off and told 'no'. I never bothered again, I was quite happy on the soft stuff that was all over the ground. It was like having a huge bed everywhere. I'd never known anything like it, I had only ever known concrete and straw. They held me by the collar and brought the cat within sniffing distance, making soft noises like I would think it was cute and cuddly or something. I couldn't see how it could possibly be part of this pack, a low creature like that which smelled funny.

I can't remember the details, but after a short while I know I did get the cat and damaged its leg. I tasted blood and was so excited that catching it was nearly worth the commotion that followed. The tall creatures shouted and raved and wailed about it and I was terrified. I suppose I should admit here and now that I am a bit of a softie deep down and don't like confrontation and certainly don't like being shouted at or hit.

The next thing I knew I was back in a kennel. I was devastated. I was just starting to adjust to the new life, and there I was in a rather dingy cell. I had got used to my new soft bed and nice meals. I had been taken for long regular walks on the lead and was happy with those. I was brushed and stroked and had certainly got used to that. I'd even got a little more used to living with the tall creatures. The down-side was that I didn't know why they sometimes shouted at me or biffed me on the nose, and, of course, the dreadful cat, the cause of my demise.

The new kennels were noisy, with a lot of barking. The food was not terrible, but was a real mixture, like you had to have whatever the tall creatures could rustle up. It wasn't what a rather delicate stomach really wanted. There was as much water as you wanted whenever you wanted and that was important. So after my initial confusion and disappointment I settled down, and got lots of sleep time which was fine by me. At least I was left in peace in my own cell. I am fairly easy going and can get used to most things, and I started to relax after a short time, as the routine was always the same. I like a routine and nothing was demanded of me, there were no great expectations. I missed the cuddles and the soft floor and the nice bed, but there were some good tall creatures at the kennels as well. They made a bit of a fuss of me and took me out for a walk in some fields that surrounded the kennels. It was a great place for walks.

There were a few other types of beast at this place. They lived outside. I walked past the ones with beaks and wings and darted at them to frighten them. The tall creatures kept me on a short lead, but still it was fun seeing the winged fellows' reactions, all fluttering around in a panic. I barked at them because I don't like them any more than cats. They are both so low in the creature chain of life that they are hardly worth the ground they take up. Okay, I suppose

I was a bit arrogant, but what is a fellow to do with breeding like mine? To be honest, most of the creatures in this place were not worthy of my company, so I ignored them. The ones with cloven feet though, they were a bit frightening. I shied away when they came near the fence that kept them safely shut in. When I walked by they called out in their peculiar language, but I understood alright. They thought I was a conceited dandy. I barked back ferociously, only because I knew they couldn't get me. Anyway, if you were as pig-ugly as them I suppose you'd be upset as well.

I need to know where I am sleeping every night, with a reasonable bed to sleep in, when my food is coming, plus some good, kind pack members. I got all of that and soon forgot the other places where I had lived. In fact, I began to forget my previous life, except that I knew I had to be wary, that other creatures can hurt you or behave in an unpredictable manner. It can make a fellow a trifle nervous if you don't know what to expect.

I soon picked up on the fact that a lot of dogs came and went in these kennels, and it was nothing to do with running and racing.

Every so often the big doors at the front of the kennels would swing open and hordes of the tall creatures would tramp in and out looking at us in our cells. There was always a lot of barking. I think some of the dogs were mad. I hated all the commotion and noise and tried to ignore it and sleep through it. Sometimes someone would stop and stare at me and keep calling my name like an idiot, the name being displayed outside of my cell. I occasionally went to see them and sniff them at the metal door, but mostly just stayed in my bed well back from them. It wasn't that I was unsociable, though I can take company or leave it, but it all seemed a waste of time. Something like racing around in a circle; not worth the effort. I don't want to give the impression that I'm lazy, well not much anyway.

Sometimes I could hear a lot of excited conversation outside another dog's cell, and before you knew it they were the dogs who had been taken away. I was envious sometimes, wondering if they had gone to a place like the building with luxury floors and big beds and sofas to lie on, and their own pack to live with.

But the chosen dogs went and another would come in and I'd get to know them and their bark. I didn't like some of them and when I was taken out and walked past their cells I would bark like the devil and growl at them. I could dish it out just as well as them, and no one was going to boss me around from now on. Like that little Jack, he would come to the metal door of his cell and growl as if to warn or frighten me off. I jumped towards him and snarled and he fled to the back of his cell. But it was just play acting; I am not an aggressive dog unless provoked. The two-legged female that I liked the best at the kennels would pull gently at my lead and say something ineffective like 'no, Jake' and coo at Jack, oh how cute he was, but I was jealous and told him in no uncertain terms to back off. He would cower in the back of his cell when I walked past after that. But there were some I would have liked to make friends with. Like Honey, I would have liked to get to know her, I mean really get to know her! Oh, the scent drove me mad sometimes. But she went the way of the others, I don't know where. I hoped she had found a good pack.

I saw life here as I'd never experienced it before. There were some tragic cases that were brought in. As I was led out for my daily walk in the fresh air I would see a scrap of fur lying at the back of a cell, matted coat, or bald coat, or running yellow eyes or sores on their legs. Sometimes it would be very tense around the place when there was a panic over somebody in one of the cells. You learn to switch off and ignore the goings on. I assumed that this was now my life, my home. It really wasn't that bad.

I lived in the kennels through the heat and then began to realise that as it got darker it got colder. The kennels were kept warm but it was dim and dreary all the same. At this colder time I became vaguely aware of the same voices saying my name on two or three different occasions. I was by now so bored with the times when the tall creatures visited and I just ignored these as I did all the others. One day however my routine was disturbed. One of the regular females came to my cell at an odd time with a lead. I was so excited to be going outside for the second time that day that I chased my tail and ran around in circles. I always did that when I was being taken out or when I knew food was coming. Whizzing round in circles could break the monotony.

I looked in at the other resident Greyhound, a ragged white female who had been there almost as long as I had. She was quiet and just sat in her basket most of the time looking sad. I couldn't resist showing off a bit to the others. So many times it was they who were taken out at odd times and not me. Jack growled at me and I snarled back, ha, nobody had chosen him yet either. I jumped back as a big black ugly dog barked and rattled his metal cell door. The white greyhound looked at me with disdain. She was a lot older; I was still very young and had much to learn. So out I bounced, and my learning began.

I'm not sure what I had expected, but to my astonishment I had to meet some tall creatures. That pulled me up a bit. They were like any other strangers and I was nervous. They tried to give me a treat, a chewy stick, which I usually gulp down, but I was too worried by this odd break in routine and I didn't want it. Besides, I had thought I might be going for a walk, which in fact is exactly what we did.

There were two strangers and one of them took my lead. I enjoyed the walk, but had to keep checking that the tall creature who I saw on most days, and who I had started to think of as my pack leader, was coming as well. I didn't want any nasty surprises. Well, it was all a bit of an anti-climax and after the tall creatures had made a lot of ridiculous fuss and tried to give me another treat I was taken back to my cell. The white greyhound looked down her long nose silently as I walked back past her, much more subdued than when I went out. The ugly black dog barked madly and Jack jumped up and down at his door. I was glad to get in and lay down quietly to wait for dinner.

Not long after that the same tall creatures came again. This time I was taken to the big fenced field. That was exciting as another dog was being taken out at the same time. I didn't know him, but he looked like a fussy little thing that made a lot of noise and was pulling on his lead all over the place. I never pulled on the lead because it was a waste of time. You weren't going anywhere and it just hurt your neck. He was taken to the other fenced-off paddock in the field with some other tall two-legs. My pack leader let me off the lead and I ran backwards and forwards by the fence trying to chase the other dog. The tall creatures kept calling me but I didn't know what for, so I ignored them and sniffed around the field for a bit. A smaller two- legged male threw something and gesticulated madly at it. We all stood looking at it in an awkward silence. I began to wonder whether they wanted me to race again or something equally stupid. It also occurred to me as I watched the other dog being taken back towards the kennel that they might be taking it away, and I might be taken away as well. In a panic I decided I wanted to go in, away from the uncertainty. I went and stood by the gate that led out of the field and whined while the tall creatures stood staring at me. It was kind of bizarre. I was relieved when my pack leader took me back indoors again.

2

All was normal for a while, and then the same thing happened again. This time I went for a walk around the much bigger field with no less than five tall creatures. I recognised one of them, a female who seemed to be becoming a regular, and I decided I could trust her and enjoyed my extra walk. They all made a fuss and gave me treats, and this time I rather enjoyed it. It all seemed to be safe enough and I always met up with my pack leader again and was taken back to my cell. But I was in for a shock.

The next time they came there were two of them. It was the tall female and the smaller male. I was taken into a building and there was some talk and I stood around waiting for another extra walk. However, I was taken to a big red metal thing. Of course, I had encountered these things before. They made a funny noise and moved at some speed, but I had been in the kennels for so long by then that I had completely forgotten about them. They opened a door and I think I was supposed to get in. I looked around desperately, pulling back, but could see no sign of the kennel pack leader. My heart started to race and I was scared, but at the same time felt that these creatures meant me no harm. I just didn't understand what on earth was going on. Were they taking me away? Well, I soon found out that they were.

The tall female was gentle but pretty firm. She gave the other one the lead through a grille inside the big metal box, and he pulled while she got hold of my back legs and lifted me into it. She obviously wasn't frightened of me. While I was dithering, trying to decide what I should do, I struggled and she simply got hold of my legs and I'm afraid to say that I gave in and she won. I sensed right from the start that this tall creature was having no nonsense. The tall creatures jumped into another compartment of the box and the noisy contraption moved slowly down the long lane away from the kennels. The machine was big enough to stand up in and I turned around, watching the only home I knew recede away from me.

I was frantic on that journey to what I now know was my new home. But I had no idea what was going to happen. I was taken from the vehicle through the door of another large building. Well, I was astonished. It had a soft floor for one thing. It was something like the building I had lived in before with the tall creatures. I immediately went to mark it and the female said 'no' while gently nudging me away from whatever I was going to mark. I know what 'no' means and I put my leg down pretty quickly. I then thought I was going outside and walked into something solid that I could see through. Of course, it was the big window that looks out onto my territory, I know that now. I was then taken through a passage to that territory outside, to a small area with trees and grass, and I was able to mark it happily.

It was all so strange, but I was kind of hopeful. Especially as back inside I could lie down on the soft floor covering and get some rest. I was exhausted and very grateful that I was left in peace for a while. Sometime after that the tall female gave me the best meal I'd had in ages. Things were looking up.

But then it became scary again as other tall creatures came into the building. I wondered when I would be taken back to my cell. But I wasn't taken back. Thankfully I was left in peace, except that the young male two legged creature kept fussing a little too much. I didn't know what his motives were and I hadn't worked out everyone's place in this setup yet. I wanted to stay close to the female who had lifted me into the moving machine. I had met her a few times now and sensed that I could trust her. She had given me a lovely meal and led me to a large padded bed.

I did not try it at first, unsure of where I should be or what I should do, whether the bed was just for me and whether I would be staying.

There was a noisy box in the room with lots of their language and noise going on. I vaguely remembered that from the other place I had lived. It was so different from the kennels, and there were no other barking dogs. The food, though, it was just amazing. I soon found that the new pack was always eating. Wow and did they eat! There was often someone in the small space where all the food seemed to be. It got nice and warm in there too, and from the beginning I liked to lie and watch them by the door that led to this small space with the mouth- watering smells. I realised straight away that I wasn't to touch their meals which was fair enough, they didn't come near mine. But the best thing was that I got some bits of theirs with my dinner afterwards. I couldn't believe my luck.

I soon learnt to hang around whenever they ate anything. Better still, the younger ones in the pack tried to make friends with me by giving me bits of their nice treats. I could fool them easily by looking friendly and imploringly at them. After the treat, and when there was no more coming my way, I could be unsociable again and lay in my bed. It was easy, and I wasn't yet ready to become best pals with everyone.

I was let outside frequently and was praised just for doing a wee. When it became dark the tall creatures all disappeared up the hill, like they had done in that other place. It was quite bizarre. They left me alone in a large space, which wasn't a caged kennel cell, and closed a solid door. I could hear them moving around somewhere above me. I stood rigidly listening out for danger or a nasty surprise and cried a bit. I scratched the door a couple of times but it became silent and I gave up.

I retired to my new luxurious bed. It was so cushioned and cosy, but there were no sides to restrict me like the basket I had had at the kennels, and I lay out with my legs stretched over the soft floor covering for the first time in a long time. It was wonderful. I was so tired that I probably barely moved.

As light came, I could hear the tall creatures stirring again above me which was very weird. To start with I couldn't understand why I couldn't hear the other dogs, until I remembered that I was no longer in the kennels. I got up and looked around. I sniffed everything and waited by the door. A big male opened the door and let me outside to do my business. Then the tall female arrived and gave me some more nice food. That was a relief; it looked like I was going to be fed. I looked around for a bit, it seemed that I was free to go where I wanted. There were plenty of new smells and things to explore in the small outside area, but I couldn't concentrate. I needed to know what was going to happen next. What was going to happen was that after food the female took me for an outing.

We set out along the hard surface with the moving contraptions whizzing past us. I was pretty frightened and a lot of the new noises and people around made me jump, but at least we soon got to some real walking country. It was fantastic to be out and I started to enjoy it. I didn't realise then of course, but this was going to be a regular walk for me in the future. I would in time run free across these fields and meet friends and learn to play with other dogs. That was all some way ahead.

We went back to the building and I lazed about all day on my new bed. Sometimes I moved over to look through the invisible wall to the outside. The sun streamed through and I collapsed and savoured the warmth and the rug. I could not remember ever bathing in the sun before. I was still exhausted from all the excitement and nerves from the day before. Everyone except the tall female went away and I had no idea if they would be back. She stayed with me and I was pleased because I already liked her and did not want her to leave me. She did leave me, but not for long. Later I went for another walk, this was a bonus, and then dinner again. This was great. But I'd been in this position once before and I didn't trust anything or anyone.

However, some time passed and all was peaceful and I was not taken away. I watched carefully, and soon found out who was where in the pack. Big female was pack leader and that was fine by me. I wasn't sure about the big male yet. He was above me or equal at the very least. I probably wouldn't argue with him. Small female was next. She was alright, though she was not there so much and didn't feed me, so it took longer to get to know her. Small male, well, he was bottom of the pack. I just knew it, but the trouble was he didn't seem to know it. I had to teach him. He would suddenly jump right next to me and keep calling me. He had these strange things that rolled along the floor and fluffy things he kept throwing around. They made me very nervous and freaked me out. He was a nuisance, just like some of the little annoying dogs in the kennels. I put him in his place pretty quickly and growled angrily at him. I am sorry about this now. How could I know he was a young puppy who wanted to play with me? I didn't understand what play was. I have to admit it took me rather a long time to relax and get on with him and enjoy a game. You'll be pleased to know we play all the time now and, anyway, the small male has grown into a large male in the years I have been with him. Even so, he is still way below me in the packing order.

More time passed. I was not taken back to the kennels and began to forget and feel happier. A routine emerged. The timetable that began on that first day was established. As light came, big male let me outside and gave me a biscuit. Then I settled down until the pack leader came down the hill and we had a small meal. I was taken for a great walk by the pack leader. We visited a different place every day, sometimes we went somewhere in the moving contraption but more often not. Everyone had left the building by the time we got back from our walk. I would follow pack leader as she did what she had to do. Then she would disappear up the hill for a while and when she came down I knew she was going to leave. I knew that because she would open a door to somewhere I never went and came out with a coat. Also in this dark little place were the treats. I would get a chew stick or a pig's ear or another treat and then she would leave the building.

I was then left in peace for some time, except that occasionally small female was around. She sometimes stroked my head and brushed me, I liked that, and I liked her. She was quiet and gentle, unlike the puppy,   although at two I was not much out of puppyhood myself. When the pack leader was out I was happy with the underlings on the whole, apart from small male. But when pack leader was in I just wanted to be with her. I stayed with her all the time. The others tried to tempt me to sit with them, but I wasn't interested. I felt that at last I had found my leader, found my pack. She was the one I would answer to.

On the whole, tall creatures are good. I had known them and been among them from day one. But you have to remember they are not dogs. You should not try and treat them as such. A dog has to try and understand the way of the two-legged ones, and unpredictable behaviour is quite common. They all have some funny habits and the pack I adopted was no exception. There were so many strange noisy things about the place that it took a while to get used to them and not panic. There was this thing pack leader pushed around on a fairly regular basis, often after first walk and before she went out. It lived in the place where the coats and treats were. The noise from it was shocking, louder than the moving machines outside that we got from place to place in. She pushed and pulled it all over the floor and I scooted right out of its way. I feared at first that it was an alien coming after me. To be honest I've never got used to it and have always hated it. Then in the area where the food was there was a humming machine. That was fairly benign, but the other thing which looked similar made another type of high whining noise. It was very peculiar, but after a while it just became part of the general background noise. There was a fair bit of background noise that a fellow had to try and sleep through.

After I had been there some time another tall creature visited the building. I was always better with visitors when I was with one of my pack and the visitor let me sniff them without a lot of excitement. Then we would allow them to enter our territory and I would lose interest and lay down for some kip. By now I was on sentry duty and prepared for a fight should anything threaten the pack. This visitor was no threat but came and went with great irregularity. I didn't much like this. I liked my new routine and didn't know where this one belonged. She lived in a space somewhere else in the building when she was around, and I soon decided she belonged at the bottom, even below small male.

She took me for some walks, or tried to. I wasn't going anywhere with this inferior underling, what on earth did she think? Honestly, sometimes the stupidity of these creatures is astounding. It did become rather amusing though. After a long time in my new home had passed, and when I realised she was harmless and finally, if reluctantly, accompanied her on an outing, I led her merry dance many times. I would walk happily out with her as if I was seriously going to enjoy a walk, and before we'd got to the fields I would just stop and not move. She could not move me whatever she did. I sank onto my strong haunches and did not budge. She would stand stupidly looking around her and I would whine and look longingly back towards my building and pack leader until she gave up and took me home.

She once took me to the big green area where I could run and run. (This was quite a long time after I had first arrived and pack leader let me run loose in certain places, of which more later). This day, bottom of the pack tall creature made the mistake of letting me off the lead as if she was pack leader with some kind of authority. I ran off and she came after me shouting my name, and I stopped and pretended

27

to be interested in something in the longer grass at the side of the field. As she approached I could see her out of the corner of my eye, all relieved and sighing and happily saying my name. She was just about to grab my collar and I ran off again. It was hilarious. I kept this up for a while, and eventually got bored and went home without her.

Home. I began to think of it as my home. It was by now the very cold part of the year, but here was I living in luxury like I'd never known. I even had a smart new jacket which kept me warm when we went out, and dry when it rained. Pack leader would not let me stay in when it rained though. I was reluctant to get my paws wet, but she just led me along, no arguing with it whatever the outside conditions. I did like getting out each day once I'd made the effort to move. There were just so many new scents to find and interesting places to do my business. After the walk I was allowed to sleep. And boy did I sleep. I don't understand the constant activity of the tall creatures. They are slightly mad I suppose. It is the same with some other dogs. What is it with them all? What on earth could be better or more important than a good kip snuggled down on a soft warm bed?

I was taken out frequently in the moving contraption. I was always a bit worried and on edge wondering where we were going. We started to visit another territory fairly regularly. I made a great friend in this other territory. There was an old tall creature who I pretty soon accepted as part of the pack. He always stroked my head and nose and gave me a biscuit. He was a kind one. Best of all was the four legged of the territory, a female smaller than me, but great fun. I think I can honestly say that she was my first canine friend and she taught me how to play. I was frightened at first, not of her, as I could see that she was obviously a nice bitch right from the start, but I didn't know what she was doing. She was pretty ancient but she barked loudly sometimes and ran around and growled as she pulled on a red thing, with small male or old male, or worse, my beloved pack leader, one of them pulling on the other end. Of course this was all play, but I didn't know that. How could I? I had no idea what play was about and I stood back in a sort of horrified fascination. Or I would go and lie down on her rug by the fire and pretend to ignore them all, but watched their antics out of the corner of my eye.

Later when I got to know her, I liked going out with her and running after her. We played chase and she seemed to like this even though I was bigger than her. When I tried this with other dogs they seemed frightened of me and would stop running. This was extremely handy with some dogs that were hostile. No one could outrun me. I would dance around them, letting them get in striking distance and then take off like a rocket and leave them standing. Anyhow, Cindy became a good friend. This is more than can be said of Matty.

Matty visited the old male's building as well with her pack leader. There only seemed to be two in their pack. But the first time I met the little dog I knew she was trouble. We initially went for a walk together on neutral ground but were both kept on a lead. This was still early days and I was wearing a muzzle at that time. She was even older than Cindy and stepped out with the demeanour of having a pretty high opinion of herself. After the walk we went back to the old male's territory and a false sense of security ensued. As soon as we got in Matty went for me. There was a bit of a riot for a minute with the tall creatures shouting and us snapping at each other. I don't know why they were shouting at me, I had a muzzle on. It should have been the little dog that had a muzzle on. I ceded all pretence of superiority, and anyway her scent was all over the building and obviously she had been there first. For ever after that first meeting I let her be top dog and we walked around each other and avoided any contact. These two dogs and their tall creatures came to my home territory sometimes. Can you believe the little one they called Matty walked over to my bed, sniffed it and then settled down and made herself comfortable in it! She would have had my dinner too, but that was a step too far. I've never encountered such cheek before or since. But I was not going to argue.

One day I was taken out with Cindy in the old male's car. "Come on, in the car," was by now a familiar command. There was just enough room for the both of us and Cindy generously shared her space. The thing was, I had been lifted into the car up until then, and yes, it must have looked a bit pathetic. It wasn't as if I was some little toy dog or something, but I had never attempted to get in on my own. This time the tall creatures called my name and patted the car and seemed to expect me to do something. I waited to be lifted in and gazed into the distance and ignored them. It's what I do when they are being silly. It wasn't until I saw Cindy leaping in and out of the car quite happily that I realised what they wanted me to do. I shrank back; I did not want to do it. I did not want to look a silly billy either, so I sniffed and danced about watching Cindy making an easy show of jumping in and out, the tall creatures urging her on. Well anyone can do that, I finally decided, and took a giant leap crashing into Cindy on the way in. I never looked back after that of course and now get in and out of all sorts of these machines without a thought.

3

My life had changed dramatically and I started to settle down. Maybe this could be a permanent arrangement.

As I've mentioned, when I went for walks in the early days I had the muzzle on. It did not bother me much as I'd had them on since I was a young pup. The pack leader began to let me off the lead sometimes in certain places and I could run free. I sprinted like the wind and it was the best feeling ever. On one of our regular walks there were lots of small fluffy rabbits, not like the play one that they used around the race track. These were real. I ran around after them like a mad thing to begin with, but soon discovered that I was unlikely ever to catch one.

They just dived into holes and hedges and got away. I soon gave up with them. Much better was running and playing with other dogs. I loved to get them to chase me. Sometimes two or three dogs would yap at my heels but, of course, none of them ever caught up with me. I would run in a big circle only to turn quickly and charge back the other way, which is when they would give up.

Sometimes when I took off with great speed towards some distant target I could hear pack leader screaming my name in panic. I don't know what her problem was. She seemed to think that I was going to attack the other dogs. I only did once or twice if they had an aggressive attitude or attacked me first. I did not like some of the bigger dogs who seemed to think I was a soft touch, and I would turn on them, more in warning than viciousness. If they had a go at me I would run away swiftly if it looked like I was on to a loser. But I never initiated any serious fights with teeth sinking into flesh or anything.

At other times on walks we would see larger creatures, the ones called deer. I would be kept on a lead, and they were the only times that I couldn't help straining to get away. Seeing deer running wild gave the most incredible feeling of excitement. I could feel it in my blood, the instinct of a thousand years taking over. I just wanted to chase and bring them down. One day I got the chance. It was some time into my new life and I was now allowed to run free in one or two places on our walks. Even the muzzle had taken a hike. Pack leader and I had walked for a while through some new fields and gateways where we had never been before. There was countryside stretching away in front of us. I was elated and feeling very excited and energetic. It was a dull day with a hint of rain in the air. Pack leader never let me loose in new places usually, but this time she made the mistake of letting me go free. Almost immediately I sniffed the air and picked up a scent, looked up and saw two deer in the distance. They too looked up from their grazing and for a second we stared at each other. They ran. I ran. I vaguely heard pack leader shout my name, but I was already gone and I wasn't going to stop, couldn't stop.

I ran the fastest I could and in seconds was at the end of the fields. I could see a deer far away, across a track and into another field. They had split up when I started chasing, and I picked up the scent of one of them and ran for miles. I had no notion of time or distance and I revelled in the pursuit. I hunt by sight essentially, but that doesn't mean we Greyhounds don't have the strong sense of smell as well. My blood was pumping and I sprinted backwards and forwards along a trail until I was sure I had the right scent.

It wasn't until I noticed that it was getting a bit darker and colder that I first became concerned about where pack leader might be. I was weary by now and knew I had gone far, but I also knew instinctively that I could find my way back. I had a last look around the woods where I had ended up after the chase, I had lost the scent and the deer had escaped. They were just lucky this time. I made the long trek back the way I had come easily enough, and I'm sure I heard a very distant voice calling my name. After quite some time I found the gate which we had first come through. I couldn't get back through the two other closed gates we had gone through so I had to go a long way around, but even so, I knew this was where we had started. I was tired and wet and dirty from the small stream I had dived through in my excitement. However, when I got back to the last closed gate there was no sign of pack leader or the car she had brought me in. I stood utterly exhausted and began to feel dejected. But this had to be the place she would be, surely she hadn't abandoned me. Just as I was beginning to panic she went past the gate in the car, screeched to a halt and came flying back backwards. She leapt out of the car and ran towards me saying my name over and over. Anyone would think I'd been gone for hours!

I had to have a wash down when I got back when all I wanted was my dinner. Pack leader seemed to be a bit cross. Oh well, I couldn't understand her every mood. I slept very well that night. It had been a perfect day, the like of which I'd never had. First the hunt followed by a great meal, and then collapsing on my bed for a long sleep. I dreamed of chasing the deer, only this time, in the dream, I brought it down and won the prize.

The other great thing about my new home was the cats. Oh, and there are lots of cats around where I live. I hate them and always strain to get at them, while the cheeky blighters turn and stare, like they could scare me. I never did get to chase them because I was always on a lead when I saw them, as they all seemed to hang about the building areas rather than the fields. Except for when the cat that lived next door walked through my territory. The nerve of this one was something else. He wore a bell around his neck and thought he was very handsome and superior. The cat's whiskers indeed. I would hear the bell first sometimes and see his backside disappearing over the fence. I would go into a noisy frenzy. How dare he come into my territory with such impunity? Not any more pal. I chased him off every time if I saw him when I was outside but I never caught him. Cats are so annoying the way they can escape by jumping onto a high wall, fence or tree. It drove me mad, especially when they sat there and stared at me from their high and mighty position. Being a greyhound, I might have made the fence, maybe even cleared it, but our territory was surrounded by tall trees as well.

Then there were the ones called squirrels. They came and went through the trees as well, but they were harmless and a bit boring so I didn't bother with them, though Cindy seemed to think they were worth a game. The winged creatures that visited my territory were just baffling. You'd never stand a chance of catching one, the way they took off into the air. But it was fun. It was all fun.

I gradually began to learn about fun. The pack had these fluffy toys and things that made a high screech when I chewed them. The first time it happened I dropped it and scooted to the other side of the room. As I said before, I didn't bother with them at first, I couldn't see the point and they were scary. It was Cindy who taught me that playing with toys could be fun. I watched her with disdain as she pulled and chased these things. I was puzzled and disappointed when pack leader played with her, and a bit jealous, she seemed so happy. Then one day I started to play with Cindy as well and I felt happy too. I stopped worrying that this might all lead to a fight. Cindy looked fierce and aggressive, but it was not real. Once I understood this I could join in.

So it was the same with the toys at home. I pounced on the squeaky toy and it could have been a cat. I started to enjoy myself and ran backwards and forwards in and out of the big room. The rest of the pack laughed and chased me; they thought I had gone mad. I got a lot of attention so kept doing it, and the squeaky toy turned into the cat next door and I squashed the living daylights out of it. Then I got a raggy toy and started shaking it about. Small male pulled on the other end like he did with Cindy. My teeth were stronger than his arms which was satisfying.

We carried on for a while until small male threw himself on the floor and I ran around him pretending to nip at him. It was a good game.

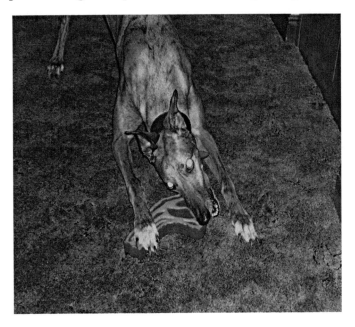

Later on when playing was a part of my life, big male was the best one for a game. He would sink into his chair gazing blankly at their noisy box.

I would jump in front of him with front legs splayed out, backside and tail wagging in the air, barking at him until he played with me. He would chuck my fluffy toy and I would pounce on it and big male would try to take it back off me while I took the stuffing out of it.

When I got tired and bored with it and went to lie on my bed, the pack still kept calling me like I was a performing idiot, so I ignored them and they finally gave up. I only did things if I chose to do them, they had to learn that I was second only to pack leader. If I wanted to play, then I would make them play. If I wanted to go outside, they had to let me out. If it was time for a walk, I would whine until they got the message. It was hard work, but they were getting better. I still had to remind small male sometimes. He wanted me to chase the toys and take them back to him like Cindy did, but I didn't want to do that. Even so, it was a good time, and small male rewarded me with a lot of affection and dog chocolate drops, so I guess it was worth it.

I had a bad habit and got told off on quite a few occasions. Well, we always did a wee in the kennels and this was my kennel now. A big and comfortable one admittedly, but I just forgot sometimes that I wasn't supposed to wee inside any more. Sometimes I couldn't help it when I still got really nervous about stuff, like when the wind was blowing a gale and there was this awful whistling around the building. Sometimes I needed to go out and there was no one there. This all stopped though when I started sleeping in the same space as the pack leader. It all started when I went up the hill.

I had no desire to go up the steep hill. They all went up and down all the time and disappeared up there when it was dark. One day small male thought it would be entertaining if I went up it as well. He ran up and down the bottom part calling me but I wasn't having any of that. The trouble was I was really curious because pack leader went up there. It was tempting to think I might be able to go where she was all the time. I didn't like not being with her. I knew when she went out that she would be back sometime and that didn't worry me. But I fretted if she was in the building and not with me. I followed her everywhere, because I wanted to and I felt safe.

So I went halfway up the hill in steps and lost my nerve several times. Getting back down was just too scary but even so, after a lot of dithering I went right to the top. Small male was delighted. You know, he was not so bad and he had his uses. So I explored and it turned out to be much the same as down the hill, just another lot of spaces to look around. I went everywhere and had a good look and put my nose in everything. I could see where pack leader spent some of her time and followed her. She helped me to go down the hill again. Well, once done, I followed her up and down all the time. Thinking about it now, it seems incredible that I would not go up at one time.

This posed a problem though. I wanted to be with pack leader when she went up the hill after last wee and biscuits. I tried lying in my bed but fretted something awful. I wanted to be with them up the hill. There followed quite a battle of wills. I whined and wee'd on their precious soft floor. They got mad and shut the door on me and told me in their no-nonsense voice to stay. They made my space very small at night, as if I was back in a cell in the kennels. I would wear them down I thought, and they would give in to me in the end.

They did indeed give in when I went up the hill on my own and settled down in their space. They did not send me away. Pack leader and big male slept on this interesting looking bed. It was huge and soft. I sniffed at it and put my nose in big male's face. I was told very firmly to lie down. It was my turn to compromise and I sighed happily and settled down next to the big bed. I slept near them in a blissful long and comfortable slumber thereafter. Everyone was happy with the arrangement. Honestly, why they had to make such a fuss about it I'll never know. But really, it was so easy to get what I wanted. It was the same with food; stand around looking hungry and sad at mealtimes and Bob's your uncle, there was the titbit in my bowl from one of their plates.

However, I didn't always have everything my own way. There wasn't much I could do when they took me to the place where the tall creatures look at your teeth and eyes and give you a sharp jab. I've never worked out what their game was, but as long as pack leader or big male was there and reassuring me and keeping me calm, I just gave in and accepted it. Nobody hurt me and I sensed that they were friendly. I did not like the squirt up the nose or the long thing stuck in the neck, but I supposed they must have a reason for doing it. We had several visits to this place, and once, horror of horrors, they left me there and I was put in a cell. I can't remember much about it as I seemed to have to sleep all the time. All I know is that my teeth felt smooth and clean when they came and took me home. I was so relieved when they collected me. There was still that anxiety that I might be left somewhere else.

But then they did. One day they did leave me somewhere else. It was hot and sunny again by then and I had really settled into my new life. How could they abandon me? But they had and I found myself back in a cell with a lot of barking and noise and different tall creatures and dogs.

It had all started with the disruption back at home. There was a flurry of activity and a lot of big bags standing around in the way. The pack banged about and were obviously preparing for something. Like all dogs I am sensitive to a change in the atmosphere. There was an air of excitement and agitation which set my teeth on edge, and then I was suddenly taken out of my routine and put in the car and taken away.

They left me at another kennel. I had a terrible time for a couple of days. I was so upset and nervous I couldn't eat or sleep, just prowled around the little cell crying. I was let out in the day, but it was hopeless. What about my walks? I had come to know the paths and woods and scents. I had felt the freedom that my new pack had given me; I had started to have fun. I was devastated.

Still, there is not much a dog can do in these circumstances but to accept his lot. Some dogs were going crazy and some were crying and it was just like back at the old kennels. At least, after the first shock at being abandoned had eased, I got to sleep a lot and no one hurt me. One of the tall creatures was even quite nice and kind and I began to wonder if I had a new pack leader. My heart wasn't in it though and I just lived and breathed through the days and got through them somehow. Of course, you've guessed, they hadn't abandoned me at all and came again to take me home. I forgot about the awful experience quickly and got back into the way of life I had come to know and love. The routine returned to normal.

We occasionally went somewhere else in the car, to another place where another small pack lived. This lot had no dogs, so any scraps were all for me. The first time I visited someone left a big tray of gravy within eating distance and I got the lot when they were not looking. Pack leader was not very impressed, but too bad, she was too late.

It was a long way, this place. I know when we are going on a long journey because my bed is arranged for me to settle down in, in the rear end of the car. On our walks there I first encountered the huge bank of water they call the sea. We all stood and looked at it and I didn't know what they expected me to do. I sniffed the air and it had a different scent to anything I had sensed before. It was stony at this place and hard on the paws, but there was a nice walk nearby where we always went. It was alright, not too traumatic and the older ones were kind and gave me food or biscuits like the other old male. I liked the oldies; they were calm and quiet and stroked me gently.

I know that a lot of other dogs need to be playing and walking and just doing stuff a lot, like fetching sticks and balls (pointless exercises if ever there were any) but that is not me. That is not the Greyhound way. We run like the wind, that's true, but we are on the whole quiet and stable. The majority of us walk along nicely on the lead without drama; we don't bark unnecessarily, we don't need to walk miles or round up sheep. We are forty miles an hour couch potatoes.

4

When the sun was high and warm we went away somewhere else. I got a little bored and fed up in the back of the car when it went on and on for hours. However, we eventually all piled out of it and I found myself in a strange little building. It was a bit noisy and even kind of shuddered when everybody walked around in it. But it was alright as they had brought my bed along and I was fed and taken for lots of walks. The pack was with me all the time which was great. There was the huge water again, but this time there was a nice soft sand to walk and run on. I had a great time running until I was exhausted. Pack leader went a little way into the water and called for me to go as well. I danced around; I sometimes got a bit agitated if pack leader was somewhere I could not get to. I dipped a paw in and then just splashed around a little to please her, but couldn't see what she was getting so excited about. I wasn't frightened, but didn't particularly want to stand in the cold water.

Then pack leader and big male played this game they sometimes did. Big male would hold me and pack leader would walk away until she was a speck in the distance. Then big male would let me go and I would sprint as fast as I could to catch her up. They tried to do it the other way round, but I really wasn't interested in chasing after anyone else. The sand was fantastic to run on. There was something inside me that knew its feel under my feet already. Of course, it might just have been in my memory from the race track. But I don't think so, it was in my blood and I could feel the ancestral instinct to run and chase and hunt once again. This was how life should be, running with my pack, running free.

We went to many new and exciting places, some far away and some not. I became happy and contented and even started to let small male share my space. He taught me to offer my paws. I learnt pretty quickly, even if I say so myself. It is not hard when chocolate (only dog ones, they never gave me theirs) or biscuits are on offer. I could jump up in the air to reach a biscuit in his hand, all four paws easily off of the ground. The two lowest in the pack, the female who came and went and small male, were great for extra food. They both went to their spaces with food, and I would follow them and just lay down at their feet happily staring at them as they ate. They had to share something because I looked so appealing, it was easy.

One night though I was not so clever. Small male came back from wherever he had been when it was long past dinner time and very dark. He dropped a bag of something on the little table near where I slept and went off up the hill. This was in the earlier days before I slept up the hill. After a while I thought I could smell something rather nice. I took hold of the bag and shook it. I just couldn't believe my luck, it was full of chocolate, their type of chocolate. I spent an age in blissful oblivion eating it in the dark.

When it became light however I did not feel so blissful. When pack leader saw all the paper over the floor she got really mad. She was cross with small male and obviously not pleased with me. What did she suppose? That I would not touch such a treat? I lay in my bed out of the way with my head between my paws. Needless to say I was very unwell all day. Apparently I had eaten a very dangerous substance that can kill a dog. Would I do it again? You bet. In fact I had a plate of delicious sausages once. Another time, when it was still the cold time of year after I had left the kennels, they did something very strange. They brought a tree into the building. I was tempted to lift my leg and mark it, but it was a bit too high. Not too high to sniff out the chocolate that was hanging on the tree. Perhaps it was one of their games, I don't know. I was able to reach one of the chocolates and bring the tree down. I'm always on the lookout, but unfortunately they don't leave me alone with food any more.

On the infrequent occasions when pack leader and big male were not there I was well looked after by small female. I liked her; she was a good substitute for pack leader. In fact she became pack leader when the real one was away. I was fine with that. However, when pack leader returned we all took our correct places again. I was much more amiable with bottom of the pack female now that she had learnt where she belonged. No one tried to hug me too much like they did to start with, or jump around when I didn't want to. I liked to play sometimes and they just had to wait until I wanted to. When we were with Cindy she let them do anything they pleased and she just went along with it. Well good for her, she was only a mongrel after all.

One day we went to Cindy's territory, but Cindy was not there. There was a bad atmosphere which was quite depressing. The tall creatures spoke quietly and sadly. I realised quite soon that Cindy had gone and was not coming back. I sat on her mat by the hearth. She was my best friend and she had gone. The old male stroked my head, but the touch was weak and he was sad. Maybe I helped everyone a little by being around. Matty was her usual belligerent self, though Cindy had been her only friend. Cindy was friends with everyone and I'll miss her.

I adore my tall creatures, but they remain a mystery. I cannot possibly understand all of the daily goings on in the pack's lives. But I share their lives and when I know there are upsets and sadness, or happiness and excitement, I can share that too. I can be a calming or comforting or excitable presence and add something to the perspective of their existence. When they don't need any more words or actions to add to their traumas and dramas, I can just be there.

Sometime after Cindy had gone, we went to the old male's building again and he was not there either. I could sense that pack leader was upset and I was unsettled by the heavy atmosphere once again. Another pack that I'd only met a couple of times showed up. They must have lived far away but pack leader accepted them as our own, so I did as well. I was wary of the young pup two-leggeds who were with them though. There were two who looked identical and were far too boisterous. But, happily, they were frightened of me without me having to do anything and kept well out of my way. I kept one eye on them all the same. It was a strange sort of time. While the tall creatures sat around with their low spirits, Matty and I walked around each other and kept out of each other's way, I kept away from the young two-leggeds and they kept away from me. It may not seem very amiable, but it made for a more peaceful existence. Anyhow, whatever goes on in their baffling world, a fellow still needs his dinner and his walks, sometimes better late than never.

We visited the old male's building sometimes after that, but the old male was never there again. My guess was that he'd gone to the same place as Cindy.

So, after the times of disruption, tall creatures coming and going, visits to the sea or the vet, or dogs and tall creatures suddenly disappearing, life went on and returned to normal. Pack leader was always reliable. She didn't fret about the noise the wind made, or a sudden paper whipping up around our feet when we went for a walk. She was never afraid of other creatures and dogs, she didn't jump at strange loud noises in the buildings or bother when other dogs barked loudly. I learnt to relax.

But even pack leader occasionally did something unpredictable and unsettling and she did get angry at times. I was once sleeping peacefully when there was a terrific commotion. I saw small male flash by the door and disappear up the hill with pack leader shouting like a mad thing that had lost her mind. Startled, I barked at them, joining in the general hysteria until she shoved me back into my space and shut the door. I went to my bed with my tail between my legs. I didn't like this strange aggressive behaviour at all. When things were quiet again, pack leader came and sat with me and stroked my head. That was a very rare kind of upset, but she was not happy at other times, like when I used to wet inside, or when I snapped at the heels of small male's companions. Well, what a shower they were. They didn't seem capable of speaking in quiet tones, or getting around without pushing and shoving each other and fighting. Small male was growing, and maybe he was soon going to join this other pack he roamed around with. A rough breed altogether I would say. They would dash through the doorway and run up the hill frightening me to death. The noise they made was worse than firework night, and they had these things that made such an incredible loud whining and thumping sound it was a nightmare.

When I made a show of chasing them, pack leader shouted 'no' at me and made me cower just for showing them whose territory they were messing with. Pack leader was wrong and I growled, angry with her. They could have been anyone who might want to attack her, and I wanted to protect her with my life. She should learn some sense, sometimes she did not know best.

But I even became used to them and their rough ways, and eventually left them alone and became friends with one or two of them. They all just needed to understand that I had to have time to get to know how things worked in every new situation.

5

The cold faded away for the third time since I had arrived and I was particularly happy when it began to get warmer and the surrounding countryside burst into bloom and song all around. I was older and more mature these days and I ran and played with the friends I had made. Cindy and Matty were now both gone, but there were others. There was little Kim, yapping at my legs while I leapt over and around her. There was Marge with her nose in the air, never bothering with me despite my attentions. Harvey was okay but we argued at times. Ringo and Topsy, Lucy and Cooper too. The bitches were by far my favourites.

Looking back now, I don't know that I could ever see as clearly as I might have done. How I did see was normal to me, but everything was not normal. Still, I could not know that it was going to end so badly. Pack leader, large male, small male and I, had been to another place near the sand and the sea. I was so happy and relaxed. We went for lots of walks in some great places. The scent of the warm air and all the new places to explore and the huge stretch of sand to run on made it the best time I had ever had. I could see fine, just as I always had, if not absolutely a hundred per cent.

When we got back to our own territory we settled back into the routine and everything was as it should be. I had one of the visits to the vets for a prick in the neck. It was a vet I had met before and he was ok. Everything was fine and away we went.

It was a little while after this that I found I couldn't see very well out of my right eye. It was hazy and after another little while it became extremely foggy. When out on one of our walks I walked straight into a prickly bush and yelped and pack leader called to me to come on. When we got home she noticed what the fuss had been about and, as she washed the small scratch below my right eye, I obviously could not tell her that I had not seen the prickly bush. Then, more worryingly was that the other eye became a bit hazy too. For a short time after that I would go to my water bowl and put my head down to drink and sometimes miss the bowl. I went outside and once missed the step. I was a little bemused to say the least. I knocked my nose on the door when it was unexpectedly closed. No one else seemed to notice and I wasn't too bothered, just puzzled.

Then one day I went in my usual excitement for dinner, and as pack leader put my dish down and I fumbled around before finding it, she must have suddenly noticed that I was not seeing clearly because she kept looking closely at me and especially at my eyes. There was a discussion about my having different coloured eyes, and I got a little unnerved with everybody studying them. However, my left eye seemed to get better so we all relaxed again. I started to adjust to seeing with one eye, though they didn't know that. Then quite suddenly there was another deterioration in my left eye and I could not see at all. I heard the word 'vet' again. We went for our normal walk one day and I ran headlong into a small stream. I became disorientated and didn't know what was happening. I really could no longer see at all. Just like that.

At the vets I was nervous and distressed but waited patiently to be seen. I could now just see some shadow and movement as other dogs moved around the room waiting to be seen as well. After a lot of talk over my head I was led to the cell where I had been once before. I actually settled down quite quickly, I was tired and worn out and surrendered to whatever might happen next. What happened next was that a lot of different two-legged ones came and went, took me out, shone things in my eyes. At least the good eye cleared again so I could see a little of where I was. I was just so sleepy though and past caring. I stayed for a while longer and definitely felt better by the time pack leader came for me. I knew she would not abandon me. We went home.

I bumped into things a bit at first, but as I still had some sight in one eye I did not feel too bad. We carried on as normal except that I was just a little apprehensive when we went for walks. But that was by no means the end of it. I had to go to a new place and see another person who spent much time looking into my eyes and talked a lot to big male. I was fed up with it by now and wanted to be back to my old self, running and playing and sleeping back at home. But it was not to be.

My left eye was alright for a while, but something kept happening and I could hardly see at all for a short time. Then it would clear again. It went on like that. Could see, couldn't see. For the pack it was a rollercoaster ride of joy followed by disappointment. For me, despite all that going on, my life was not affected very much. By the time I finally went blind I was fairly used to it. I got up the same, went up and down the hill the same, went outside to do my business the same, had my food and drink the same.

Of course, I knew every inch of my home territory, where everything was placed, exactly where my food and drink would be. I negotiated my way around. After all, I still had perfect hearing and smell. As long as everything was left where it had always been I just got on with it and lived as normal. If something did move or something was put down in my way it wasn't too much of a problem either. I just bumped into it once and then went around it the next time.

I never really hurt myself. For one thing, you have to move more slowly and feel your way around when you are blind. When I know there is a step coming up, I reach out with one leg first to see if I've got to the right place.

There was a heavy atmosphere about the place. Everybody was upset, far more upset than I was. In fact I got extra petting and treats, so I was pretty relaxed about it all.

Going out for a walk however was a little trickier. Pack leader kept me on a lead at first but I wanted to stop to sniff and pee as usual, which was a bit frustrating for both of us. So, as I was fine walking on the lead pack leader soon became confident enough to let me loose.

I know all the paths and tracks where we walk and just keep to those. I follow along behind pack leader quite happily, only occasionally veering into the long grass, a bush or anything else in the way. It becomes second nature to use ears and nose more. I can still lag behind, sniffing at the interesting scents, being my own dog and then trot to catch her up. She will stop and wait for me, making sure I know where she is by making noises or calling my name frequently. If there is an obstacle she will stay close and guide me round it. I still enjoy my walks except for one thing. When I meet other dogs I can't check them out, see what they are up to or know what to expect. To get around that problem, pack leader puts me on the lead and holds me close until the other dogs or people have passed by. This is much safer and we are all happier with that.

We have gradually come to terms with my blindness. The tension of the first weeks has faded and life carries on pretty much as it always has. I couldn't run after I first became blind, but one day I did run again. I knew when we had arrived at the huge empty space that was covered in flat springy grass. I knew where we once had stood to watch young male play a noisy game with a lot of other young pups and one of those balls they used to try and get me to chase. I knew it from when I'd played up with lowest in the pack and ran off home. I could probably still find my way home now. I knew it from when pack leader and I had played games chasing after each other. Now I sensed that huge space around me and I could run again, just a little way.

I will never sprint so fast again or hare around like a maniac. But I can still dance and parry and dodge past pack leader, we can still chase and play. I have complete trust in my pack that they will not lead me into anything harmful and will keep me away from hazardous situations. After all, I am still quite young and am not ready to give up yet. It is alright, life is different but good.

A being can give up or they can get up and carry on. As we set off for the morning exercise I walk along happily, ears pricked, eager to get at some unexpected scent. Sometimes it can still go wrong. Like once, when I met a large dog and I wanted to play. Forgetting for a moment that I could not see, I stretched my front legs down and out and put my bottom up and wagged my tail in the air in an attitude of play. Pack leader was not quick enough to stop me and as the dog came to me in a rather excitable fashion I darted off, straight into a bramble bush. I did scratch myself a little, but I was ok and not too fazed. Pack leader was more concerned, making a great fuss over me.

I can still feel the breeze in my coat, the sun and the rain. I can sense the kind of day it is from the atmosphere and enjoy the wonder of my own existence. I can still find and track the exciting scents around me. I can still walk, run and play. I can jump in and out of the car easily and go up and down the hill. I only stumbled once in the early stages of my blindness on my way down. It is all about gaining confidence in the new situation and having a pack you can trust to guide you. I can eat and drink and sleep. I can do everything almost the same way I have always done. When I am in blissful sleep I still chase cats.

Jake's pack leader would like to add a few words of encouragement and advice.

After a diagnosis of blindness, especially if it is sudden as in Jake's case, initially there will be disbelief accompanied by a feeling of pity for yourself and the dog. There will be tears when the dog stumbles and looks up pathetically with blank eyes. The future looks uncertain and you don't know whether you will be able to keep the dog. You will grieve for what you both have lost, a walk-mate, a playmate, a companion who will now be entirely dependent on you. Questions will come to mind with no answers and no one to answer them. Will your happy independent pet become depressed and unable to be left? Will you ever be able to go away with him or take him anywhere again? Is there an underlying condition that has caused the blindness which will cause other problems?

In our experience, although most vets are happy to try and help and to answer questions, there is little they can advise other than 'dogs adapt well to blindness'. This is indeed true, but neither you nor the vet can know how you or the dog is going to cope or adapt at first. We did have some time to adjust while Jake had partial sight and it is much easier if a dog goes blind slowly, as in age related sight loss.

Retinal detachment is the cause of Jake's blindness. The dog feels no pain and there are no warning signs. Jake had his annual check up two weeks before we first noticed something was wrong. Unfortunately, there is no treatment for this condition. Having had tests for various conditions which can cause blindness and all those tests being negative, Jake's blindness was probably caused by an autoimmune response which led to the retina becoming detached.

Loss of vision can be caused by many things including hereditary genetic conditions, diabetes (indirectly), cataracts, glaucoma, trauma to the head and tumours. Parasites, bacterial and viral infections can also affect the eyes.

A veterinary eye specialist needs to be consulted in the case of blindness. Your regular vet will refer you.

Dr. David Gould is one of only seven recognised RCVS Specialist in Veterinary Ophthalmology. He saw Jake and initially treated him with steroids to try to save the left eye which still had partial vision. I was confused by all of the different retinal conditions that I read about while researching canine blindness and asked for clarification which he kindly gave.

Dr.Gould advises:

PRA (Progressive Retinal Atrophy), retinal dysplasia, retinal detachment and SARDS (Sudden Acquired Retinal Degeneration) are all different distinct conditions. Retinal degeneration is a general term, rather than a distinct condition, that develops as a consequence of the diseases listed above. However, whilst PRA, retinal detachment and SARDS will always lead to retinal degeneration, retinal dysplasia does not always do so, depending on the severity of that condition.

The main causes of blindness in dogs depend very much on the breed. Common causes are cataracts, glaucoma and retinal degeneration (of any cause e.g. one of the above conditions), but there are many other causes too.

Jake's condition is retinal detachment with a number of possible causes, the most common being:
- *Inherited – this is unlikely because of Jakes age (which by the way was five when he became blind)*

- *Secondary to high blood pressure (ruled out by Jake's normal blood pressure readings)*
- *Head trauma (none)*
- *Autoimmune disease (most likely though unproven; such investigations require a lot of expensive tests)*

Cataracts are treatable and are not life threatening or painful.

Glaucoma can cause discomfort. Look out for itching, watery eyes and avoiding light. Early treatment is essential otherwise, as with humans, sight can be permanently lost.

I would strongly recommend a pet insurance plan. I was in two minds whether it was worthwhile, Jake being a fit and healthy young dog. But I decided that it would be wise just in case Jake broke a leg, or some other such thing, while he was running around at forty miles an hour! Although the insurances do not cover routine checkups and inoculations and there is an excess to pay, there are many other conditions and accidents that can strike a dog out of the blue.

We had no knowledge of canine blindness before Jake. I have discovered that there is not much coverage or advice about it, but have found some helpful web sites and books as listed below.

We have found that there are certain points to remember which can make life easier, most of them very quickly become obvious. It is helpful to leave furniture in the same position in the house. The dog knows where everything is and will negotiate his way around it. Also he knows where his food and water is and will find it easily if it stays in the same place. Doors are best left open or, if that is not practical, completely shut so that the dog will not bump into their hard edges. I read on one internet site of all sorts of tricks, like wrapping the edges of furniture in bubble wrap and putting in child safety stair gates. Putting scents on objects such as lemon furniture polish or vanilla extract, so that the dog connects the objects with the scent. We have never found the need to do anything different in our house. Jake walks around everything just as he always did, goes up and down the stairs and jumps in and out of the car, but others might find such tips helpful. Jake occasionally misjudges something, but it really is not a major problem.

That said, people and their blind dogs will all have different experiences and stories to tell.

One of the most important things to remember is not to surprise a blind dog. A sudden noise or unexpected pat on the head can startle him. Some dogs may become aggressive with their blindness and may lash out if suddenly alarmed. All new visitors should be made aware of this. Use the voice or gently stamp on the floor to let them know someone is present and then let the dog sniff the visitor before they touch him until he is happy with their presence. This is actually a good idea whether the dog is blind or not.

Outings can be more tricky. I was afraid at first that we would never have a good and relaxing walk ever again. This too proved not to be the case. Some owners will find that they cannot let the dog off the lead, but a flexi-lead is a good alternative. You can control the dog's movements while letting him explore at the same time. I now realise that it would have been helpful, while Jake was still only partially blind, to use voice and words to warn him of an upcoming change of terrain or obstacles. I do this now and it seems to work very well. I.e. if we cross the road I keep the lead short, then gently pull upwards on the collar and say 'up' as we reach the kerb. If I know there is a gate or stile coming up I stop and take hold of his collar, say 'come on then' and guide him through or around. Jake knows all of the walks we go on like the back of his paw, and I feel he is happier off the lead, following the paths and trails. I frequently talk to him so that he can follow me. Occasionally he veers off course, but we have never found this to be a serious problem, and he has only scratched himself on a bramble bush once. I would not advise this for all dogs and if we go somewhere new Jake will always be on the lead. He walks very well on the lead and trots along happily beside us. Our one biggest problem with Jake as a blind dog is other uncontrolled dogs. It may be advisable to carry a stick, as coming across the occasional aggressive loose dog can be nerve wracking for all of us.

It is all about knowing your own dog, being aware of and alert for problems that can crop up and feeling your way about the best course to take. You are not alone, the dog will make some decisions for himself and you help each other.

Jake is the only dog in the house, and there will be other issues if there is more than one dog. E.g. if he has been top dog, there may be a need to establish whether his position is going to change. If he becomes aggressive towards the other dogs it could be stressful for everyone at first. The dogs themselves will more than likely work things out, but they will need time to adjust.

But, whatever the circumstances, life does get better after the first grim few days after diagnosis. The blindness becomes normal. It is amazing what Jake can still do. Other people we meet do not realise he is blind until I tell them.

Information and support for owners of blind dogs:

www.blinddog.info A forum to discuss blind dog issues. People write with their questions and concerns, and others respond with suggestions and answers and their own experiences. This is good for anyone with a newly blind dog who is feeling isolated.

www.oldies.org.uk As the name suggests this is a website more concerned with elderly dogs and associated problems including blindness. There is a lot of good sound advice and would be useful for anyone adopting a blind dog and bringing it into a new home, which will have its own unique set of problems. Type in 'blindness' in the search box on the oldies site.

www.blinddogs.com is an American site set up and dedicated to Linda Glass who founded the site.

http://angelvest.homestead.com/ makes a white hoop for blind dogs to wear called little angel vest. Also gives advice.

www.peteducation.com A very useful site with lots of information for all pet owners. It has a dictionary of diseases and disorders and explains progressive retinal atrophy.

www.veterinaryvision.com/ Information on common eye diseases.

www.vetspecialists.co.uk Davies veterinary specialists in Higham Gobion, Hertfordshire, where Jake was treated, gives information on some procedures like cataracts, the circumstances of eye removal, and screening for inherited eye disease of pedigree dogs and bitches used for breeding. There is also information about other specialist services.

www.petcarebooks.com/ *LIVING WITH BLIND DOGS*: A resource book and training guide for owners of blind and low vision dogs by Caroline D. Levin ISBN 0-9672253-4-5, Lantern Publications, 1998, 2003

BLIND DOG STORIES: TALES OF TRIUMPH, HUMOUR AND HEROISM. A book by Caroline D. Levin

Greyhounds as rescue dogs.

The Greyhound is a breed with a history dating back at least 6,000 years. Ancient drawings and pottery designs show ancestors of the Greyhound across the Mediterranean areas from Arabia and Africa. They came from the sands of the desert where they were revered as guard dogs and hunting dogs. They have been a presence in human existence across the years, represented in art, history and sport. They are mentioned by Shakespeare in several plays, a favourite being from Henry V:

> *I see you standing like Greyhounds in the*
> *slips*
> *Straining upon the start. The game's afoot:*
> *Follow your spirit: and upon this charge*
> *Cry 'God for Harry! England and Saint*
> *George!'*

There are many paintings depicting Greyhounds, especially from the middle ages, and kings and queens incorporated Greyhounds into their coats of arms. The modern Greyhound is bred for racing, showing and is still used for coursing. This is now 'lure' coursing, since the hunting ban. The Greyhound belongs to a group of a particular type of hound known as sight hounds. As the name suggests, they hunt by sight rather than scent. This group includes the Whippet, Sloughi and Saluki (both Arabian Greyhounds, the Sloughi is smooth coated, the Saluki has feathers on legs and tails), the Scottish Deerhound, Irish Wolfhound, Afghan Hound and Italian Greyhound. Greyhounds are increasingly crossbred with other breeds like Collies, Terriers and Salukis, and the resulting Lurchers are used for hunting and coursing. Lurchers will have different characteristics from Greyhounds, having been bred for various purposes like improving stamina over distance or obedience when recalled.

So, Greyhounds are not dogs most people think of when looking for a family pet. However, they make wonderful pets and companions if given the right start when they retire from the track. Of course there is the darker side to the racing industry, where thousands of dogs are destroyed when they are no longer useful or simply abandoned, sometimes with their ears cut off to get rid of the racing registration number that is stamped inside them. But a lot of trainers now try to find homes for their retired Greyhounds.

There are already lots of good books and web sites about greyhound adoption, some of which are listed here. There are also numerous Greyhound rescue centres and these are the best places to find a Greyhound to adopt if you have never owned a Greyhound before. A representative of the rescue kennels will usually visit you at home and match a suitable dog to you and your circumstances. You can also ask them for advice and they will be happy to give you support.

There are many other animal rescue kennels around the UK, everyone will have a local one, and there are usually one or two Greyhounds waiting along with the other breeds of dogs to be adopted.

Knowing what type of dog you are adopting is important as sight hounds have particular traits. If there is one drawback with sight hounds, it is that they are bred for hunting and running, and will disappear rapidly during a chase. This deep instinct makes it difficult to let them off the lead and it may be a long time, months or maybe a couple of years, before you are sure you can trust the dog to run free. It should be remembered that farmers are allowed to shoot dogs if they believe they are harassing their livestock. Having said that, Greyhounds are usually quiet, obedient, anxious to please and loving in the home. They are used to being exercised walking on the lead and, contrary to popular belief, they do not need or in most cases want, ten mile hikes for exercise. Twenty to thirty minutes a couple of times a day should be sufficient to keep them satisfied. They truly are couch potatoes. The Greyhound does need to stretch its legs, it is a sprinter rather than a long distance hiker. A game or a dash about in the garden is ideal.

Knowing that Jake had harmed a cat when we got him, I used a muzzle until we were sure how he would react to other dogs, especially small dogs. But these points apply equally to any rescue dogs. The Greyhound is usually good with children but a large, strong dog might be too boisterous for a small child. They also have a reputation for being rather nervy dogs. This can be true, as in Jake's case. He was very nervous of playfulness from younger members of the family to begin with. Greyhounds usually cave in and hide away in a corner with tail between legs if shouted at. But they are by no means all nervous wrecks! Depending on their background and what experience of life they have had prior to rescue, they will behave like any other rescue dog.

They can also be great for elderly people, especially the more mature quieter dogs.

Greyhounds make lovely pets and it is a joy to watch their true character develop over time in their new home, away from the track or the rescue centre.

Greyhound Rescue West of England

www.grwe.co.uk

An Independent Greyhound rescue centre which covers a huge area of the UK. Their web site gives good advice and information about Greyhounds and shows dogs awaiting adoption.

Also a good on-line shop for all things Greyhound. Helpline: 07000 785092

HULA animal sanctuary
 www.hularescue.org/
Glebe Farm
Aspley Guise
Milton Keynes

There are 70 Greyhound rescue centres listed under the umbrella of the RGT, the Retired Greyhound Trust

www.retiredgreyhoundstrust.co.uk or contact at:

Retired Greyhound Trust
149a Central Road
Worcester Park
Surrey KT4 8DT   Tel: 0870 4440673

Books

Pet Owner's Guide to the Greyhound (pet owners guide series) by Anne Finch

Living with a Greyhound by Cynthia A Branigan

Retired Racing Greyhounds for Dummies (Howell Dummies series) by Lee Livingood

Greyhound Tales: True stories of Rescue, Compassion and Love by Nora Star

The Best Finish: Adopting a Retired Racing Greyhound by Carolyn Raeke

The Reign of the Greyhound by Cynthia A Branigan

Sloughi (Comprehensive owners guide) by Marie-Dominique Crapon de Caprona

Printed in the United Kingdom
by Lightning Source UK Ltd.
129483UK00001BA/151-186/P